SUKHMANI SAHEB

God is One and only One
and is present everywhere.

He is our only Support and Refuge.

The surest way to
come close to Him and be blessed
by His treasures is to constantly remember His
Name and to enshrine Him in the temple of our heart.

The company of saints (holy men)
helps you in the realisation of God and
works out our salvation—speaking ill of
them meets with God's wrath!

All worldly objects to which
man is lured by Mammon are false and
will pass away—Only God's Name is permanent.

All vices like ego,
attachment, greed, lust, anger etc.
should be resisted and overcome as they
stand between us and God and delay our salvation (liberation),
which is the ultimate goal of man's existence.

Sukhmani Saheb

Treasure of Bliss

A poetic rendering in English of
some selected verses from
SUKHMANI SAHEB

BHARAT BHOOSHAN

New Age Books

ISBN: 81-7822-258-2

First Edition: Delhi, 2005

Published by
NEW AGE BOOKS
A-44 Naraina Phase-I
New Delhi-110 028 (INDIA)
Email: nab@vsnl.in
Website: www.newagebooksindia.com

Printed in India
at Shri Jainendra Press
A-45 Naraina Phase-I, New Delhi-110 028

Dedicated

to

MY WIFE SATYA PRABHA

To whom I owe so much
and
For whose health and happiness
I pray !

ACKNOWLEDGEMENTS

I express my deep gratitude to:

- The Almighty God to whom I owe everything.

- My late Guru and parents who have always been my role models.

- Dr. Subhash Goyal, Dr. David Flynn, Dr. K.R. Singh, Dr. Prabha Thakur, Dr. Girija Vyas and Dr. Manohar Prabhakar for their appreciation and encouragement.

- My sons — Pranav and Pavitra — who went through this script and made some valuable suggestions and also other members of my family for their love, care and support.

- Mr. Narendra Prakash Jain and Mr. Rajeev Jain for publishing this manuscript.

BHARAT BHOOSHAN

CONTENTS

PREFACE

Though a Hindu by birth and faith, I have great respect for all religions.

Luckily, I was born in a family, which was both God-fearing and religious (my father being a renowned scholar of the Vedas and other Vedic literature). I was initiated by my parents into the main teachings of our ancient literature since childhood.

As I grew in this environment, which was conducive to spiritual pursuits and aspirations, I became interested in other faiths also and gradually acquainted myself with their main teachings and beliefs.

As a result, I felt convinced that despite differences in their rituals, all religions are basically one; that though paths are different, all lead to God who is One.

It was during this quest that I laid my hand on the Sukhmani, which is held in high esteem by our Sikh brethren. The more I read it and pondered over its rich content, the more I fell under its inevitable charm.

Some of the teachings, effectively and succinctly conveyed through this scripture, to the devotees are:

- *God is One and only One and is present everywhere.*
- *He is our only Support and Refuge.*
- *The surest way to come close to Him and be blessed by His treasures is to constantly remember His Name and to enshrine Him in the temple of our heart.*
- *The company of saints (holy men) helps us in the realisation of God and works out our salvation — speaking ill of them meets with God's wrath!*

- *All worldly objects to which man is lured by Mammon are false and will pass away — only God's Name is permanent.*
- *All vices like ego, attachment, greed, lust and anger should be resisted and overcome as they stand between us and God and delay our salvation (liberation), which is the ultimate goal of man's existence.*

Though the above ideas and beliefs contained in the Sukhmani Saheb did NOT strike me as entirely new (being already there in the Vedas, the Upanishads and the Bhagvadgita), what touched my heart and soul were the simplicity and directness of its approach. I was wonder struck to find how complex philosophical and metaphysical concepts have been communicated so effectively in the language of the common man. It cajoles, coaxes and gently persuades and even at times reprimands in order to get the seeker to see the truth it conveys.

I have selected some passages from the Sukhmani Saheb that resonated most with me and translated them in English in free verse. This rendering is by a layman for the layman and not for a scholar, its approach being more emotional than intellectual. There are inherent limitations and challenges of translating from one language to another, particularly of religious scriptures. Though I have made all attempts to keep close to the text and at any rate, convey the spirit as accurately as possible, if I have erred somewhere inadvertently, I seek readers' indulgence.

I will think my labour has been amply rewarded, if it succeeds in motivating or inspiring even a few to come nearer to God and read the original text of this matchless Holy Scripture.

New Delhi   **Bharat Bhooshan**

INTRODUCTION

Sukhmani Saheb, which forms an integral part of *Guru Granth Saheb*, the most revered scripture of the Sikhs, was composed by the fifth Guru of the Sikhs, Arjun Dev Ji (1563 – 1606).

The Guru is believed to have undertaken this stupendous task on the request of thousands of his devotees who wanted him to make available to them some prayer book, which they could read daily for their spiritual upliftment.

Sukhmani Saheb, which incorporates the Guru's thoughts and philosophy, is a unique composition, set in *Raag Gauri*. Composed in Gurmukhi, the language of the masses at that time, it consists of 24 *astpadis* (cantos); each preceded by a *sloka* (stave). Each *astpadi* has eight *pauris* (stanzas) — and each *pauri* has 10 lines. This structure is followed uniformly throughout with no exception. Overall it contains 24,000 words, corresponding to 24,000 breaths a person takes every day.

Different *astpadis* deal with different subjects — each *pauri* carrying forward the theme to its logical conclusion. While appearing to be loosely knit to layman, *astpadis* have remarkable thematic unity and coherence. One of the most popular and impressive of Guru Arjun Dev Ji's writings, Sukhmani Saheb is rich in poetic imagery and philosophical depth.

In *astpadi* 24, the Guru says that the devotee, through the sincere recitation and understanding of this Psalm of Peace, will be crowned with glory, both in this world and the God's court. It is believed among the Sikhs that reading of this holy scripture 51 times not only transports the devotee to a state of bliss but also helps him achieve whatever he sets his heart upon.

One might ask if *Sukhmani Saheb* was composed by Guru Arjun Dev Ji, why is it that several messages, contained in the verses are attributed to Guru Nanak Dev Ji, the first Sikh Guru? The scholars of Sikhism believe that all subsequent Gurus drew their wisdom and inspiration from Guru Nanak Dev Ji and, therefore, attributed their own thoughts to him, as a mark of their respect to him.

Guru Arjun Dev Ji, the author of the *Sukhmani Saheb*, was a legend of his times. "Coming events cast their shadows before", goes a proverb. The same proved true in case of Guru Arjun Dev Ji. He was born to Bibi Bhani and Guru Ram Das on April 15, 1563 A.D. at village Goindwal (currently in Amritsar District) in Punjab.

Soon to realise his potential were Guru Amar Das (father of Bibi Bhani) and Guru Arjun Dev Ji's father, Guru Ram Das. Noticing exceptional talent in the young Arjun Dev, they arranged for his all-round education to equip him to take the responsibility of propagating the "Word of God". He learnt Gurmukhi, Persian, Sanskrit besides philosophy, religion and other subjects from village elders including his maternal grandfather and uncle.

In view of Arjun Singh's outstanding achievements and disciplined behaviour, his father, Guru Ram Das, sidestepping the claim of his elder son, Prithi Chand, declared him his successor and the fifth Guru of the

Sikh faith on August 28, 1581, before departing for his heavenly abode four days later.

Guru Arjun Dev Ji was responsible for the concept and construction of Harmandir Saheb at Amritsar, the city founded by his father. This temple, with four doors to allow people from all the four castes, bears a testimony to the Guru's all-encompassing love for people of all castes and creeds. The temple, which took three years to complete, under his supervision, was inaugurated at the Guru's initiative by Sufi Saint Mian Mir in 1588.

To Guru Arjun Dev Ji also goes the credit of the construction of Tarn Taran at Village Khara, blessed with abundant natural beauty. There is a big pond in Tarn Taran, where a dip is believed to cure devotees of chronic diseases, including leprosy.

During the 1595 famine in Lahore, the capital of King Akbar at that time, Guru Arjun Dev Ji, along with a large number of his followers, undertook rescue and rehabilitation work. This not only endeared him to the local population, but also won respect from Akbar, who is believed to have met him during one of his visits to Punjab.

However, when Akbar died in 1605, his successor, Jahangir, turned against the Guru after his ears were poisoned by Chandu, a minister in his court. Chandu's proposal for marriage of his daughter with the Guru's 11-year-old son, Hargobind, was rejected by the Guru. Chandu sought revenge against the Guru by projecting him as an enemy of Islam. He managed to persuade Jahangir to order that the "home and hearth of the Guru be confiscated and he be killed after torture in keeping with the Royal Law."

After torturing the Guru for five days in various ways, Jahangir's men threw him in river Ravi putting an end to his life on May 30, 1606. The Guru remained firm and kept repeating God's name till the end, displaying exceptional forbearance, courage and faith in God. The Guru's martyrdom is observed with great reverence and piety symbolising his supreme sacrifice on the altar of Truth.

TEXT & TRANSLATION

सिमरउ सिमरि सिमरि सुखु पावउ
कलि कलेस तन माहि मिटावउ ।
Simaru simar (i) simar (i) sukh (u) pavau.
Kal (i) kales tan mah (i) mitavau.

सिमरउ जासु बिसुंभर एकै
नामु जपत अगनत अनेकै ।
Simrau jas (u) bisunbhar ekai.
Nam (u) japat aganat anekai.

सुखमनी सुख अंम्रित प्रभ नामु
भगत जना कै मनि विस्राम।
Sukhmani sukh anmrit prabh Nam (u).
Bhagat jana kai man (i) bisram.

प्रभ कै सिमरनि गरभि न बसै
प्रभ कै सिमरनि दूखु जमु नसै ।
Prabh kai simran (i) garbh (i) na basai.
Prabh kai simran (i) dukh (u) Jam (u) nasai.

प्रभ कै सिमरनि कालु परहरै
प्रभ कै सिमरनि दुसमनु टरै ।
Prabh kai simran (i) kal (u) parharai.
Prabh kai simran (i) dusman (u) tarai.

Remember, remember God's Name
remember it over and over again,
To rid yourself of afflictions,
sorrows and pain !

Praise and ever praise
the One God, Protector
of this universe
and cherished by all !

The Almighty Lord, Bestower
of all happiness,
resides in the temple
of a devotee's heart !

With rememberance of God,
birth — rebirth cycle halts
ending the fear of Yama,
the God of Death !

Not only the fear of Death,
but also the enemies
run away from him
who chants God's Name !

प्रभ सिमरत कछु बिघनु न लागै
प्रभ कै सिमरनि अनदिनु जागै ।

Prabh simrat kachh (u) bighan (u) na lagai.
Prabh kai simran (i) an-din (u) jagai.

प्रभ कै सिमरनि भउ न बिआपै
प्रभ कै सिमरनि दुखु न संतापै ।

Prabh kai simran(i) bhau na biapai.
Prabh kai simran(i) dukh(u) na santapai.

प्रभ कै सिमरनि रिधि सिधि नउ निधि
प्रभ कै सिमरनि गिआनु धिआनु ततु बुधि ।

Prabh kai simran(i) ridh(i) sidh(i) nau-nidh.
(i) Prabh kai simran (i) gian (u) dhian
(u) tat(u) budh(i).

प्रभ कै सिमरनि होइ सु भला
प्रभ कै सिमरनि सुफल फला ।

Prabh kai simran(i) hoe su bhala
Prabh kai simran(i) suphal phala.

प्रभ का सिमरनु सभ ते ऊचा
प्रभ कै सिमरनि उधरे मूचा ।

Prabh ka simran(u) sabh te ucha.
Prabh kai simran(i) udhre mucha.

Rememberance of God
keeps off all obstacles,
making the devotee
ever vigilant and awake !

As he keeps chanting
God's pious Name,
fears do not overpower him
or sorrows afflict !

On such a devotee,
God bestows His nine treasures,
ridhi, *sidhi*, knowledge
and power of discretion !

Whatever comes your way
is for your good;
remembering God, you always
get the best deal!

Highest of the High
is God's Name
which liberates
many a soul !

प्रभ कै सिमरनि त्रिसना बुझै
प्रभ कै सिमरनि सभु किछु सुझै ।
Prabh kai simran (i) trisna bujhai.
Prabh kai simran (i) sabh (u) kichh (u) sujhai.

प्रभ कउ सिमरहि से धनवंते
प्रभ कउ सिमरहि से पतिवंते ।
Prabh kau simreh se dhanvante.
Prabh kau simreh se pat (i) vante.

प्रभ कउ सिमरहि सि बेमुहताजे
प्रभ कउ सिमरहि सि सरब के राजे ।
Prabh kau simreh se bemuhtaje.
Prabh kau simreh se sarab ke raje.

प्रभ कउ सिमरहि तिन आतमु जीता
प्रभ कउ सिमरहि तिन निरमल रीता ।
Prabh kau simreh tin atam (u) jita.
Prabh kau simreh tin nirmal rita.

प्रभ कउ सिमरहि तिन अनद घनेरे
प्रभ कउ सिमरहि बसहि हरि नेरे ।
Prabh kau simreh tin anad ghanere.
Prabh kau simreh baseh Har (i) nere.

God's Name quenches
Man's thirst
for wordly desires and
makes him an enlightened soul !

Rememberance of God
also makes him truly rich
and helps him
keep his honour !

No more has he
to depend on others,
God makes him
true ruler of all !

Through God's rememberance,
man gains control over his mind
and his life becomes
simple and pure !

Unlimited pleasures
he enjoys,
coming closer and closer
to his Creator !

प्रभ कै सिमरनि कारज पूरे
प्रभ कै सिमरनि कबहु न झूरे ।
Prabh kai simran (i) karaj pure.
Prabh kai simran (i) kab-hu na jhure.

जह मात पिता सुत मीत न भाई
मन ऊहा नामु तेरै संगि सहाई ।
Jah mat pita sut mit na bhai.
Man uha Nam (u) terai sang (i) sahai.

जह महा भइआन दूत जम दलै
तह केवल नामु संगि तेरै चलै ।
Jah maha bhae-an dut jam dalai.
Tah keval Nam (u) sang (i) terai chalai.

जह मुसकल होवै अति भारी
हरि को नामु खिन मांहि उधारी ।
Jah muskal hovai at (i) bhari.
Har (i) ko Nam (u) khin mah (i) udhari.

अनिक पुनहचरन करत नही तरै
हरि को नामु कोटि पाप परहरै ।
Anik punah-charan karat nahi tarai.
Har (i) ko Nam (u) kot (i) pap parharai.

All his goals
are realised,
never does he
come to grief !

When deprived of the presence
of your mother, father or a friend,
God will be your companion
taking care of you !

When ministers of Death
are after your life,
God will be there
to come to your rescue !

When your difficulties
are insurmountable,
God will instantly
lend His Hand !

When acts of expiation
yield no result,
God will free you
of million sins !

अनिक माइआ रंग तिख न बुझावै
हरि का नामु जपत आघावै ।
Anik maia rang tikh na bujhavai.
Har (i) ka Nam (u) japat aghavai.

जिह मारगि इहु जात इकेला
तह हरि नामु संगि होत सुहेला ।
Jih marag (i) ih (u) jat ikela.
Tah Har (i) Nam (u) sang (i) hot suhela.

हउ मैला मलु कबहु न धोवै
हरि का नामु कोटि पाप खोवै ।
Hau maila mal (u) kab-hu na dhovai.
Har (i) ka Nam (u) kot (i) pap khovai.

जिह पैडै महा अंध गुबारा
हरि का नामु संगि उजीआरा ।
Jih paidai maha andh gubara.
Har (i) ka Nam (u) sang (i) ujiara.

जहा पंथि तेरा को न सिञानू
हरि का नामु तह नालि पछानू ।
Jaha panth(i) tera ko na sinjanu.
Har (i) ka Nam (u) tah nal (i) pachhanu.

When countless pleasures
do not quench your thirst,
God's Name will ensure
true fulfillment !

As you walk alone
on a lonely road,
God's Name will be your
sole guide !

The filth of ego
is never wiped off,
but through God's Name,
it will go, with million other sins !

When your path is
engulfed in darkness,
God will guide you
with His own Light !

When nobody knows you
on the way,
God's Name will be
your sure identity !

जह महा भइआन तपति बहु घाम
तह हरि के नाम की तुम ऊपरि छाम ।
Jah maha bhae-an tapat (i) bahu gham.
Tah Har (i) ke Nam ki tum upar (i) chham.

जहा त्रिखा मन तुझु आकरखै
तह नानक हरि हरि अंम्रितु बरखै ।
Jaha trikha man tujh(u) akarkhai.
Tah Nanak Har(i) Har(i) anmrit(u) barkhai.

हरि का नामु दास की ओट
हरि कै नामि उधरे जन कोटि ।
Har (i) ka Nam (u) das ki ot.
Har (i) ka Nam (i) udhare jan kot.

हरि जन कै हरि नामु निधानु
पारब्रहमि जन कीनो दान ।
Har (i) jan kai Har (i) Nam(u) nidhan (u).
Parbrahm (i) jan kino dan.

पारजातु इहु हरि को नाम
कामधेन हरि हरि गुण गाम ।
Parjat(u) eh(u) Har(i) ko Nam(u).
Kamdhen Har(i) Har(i) gun gam.

When consumed with
unbearable heat,
God's Name will provide
shadow and relief !

When insatiable desires
make you thirsty,
God will shower ambrosial
drops of His Name !

God's Name is man's
Refuge and Support;
it has saved
millions of souls !

God's Name is man's
true wealth, but only one
whom God chooses,
will get it as His gift!

God's Name is like mythical
Kalpataru or *Kamdhenu*
having powers
to fulfil all desires !

मन हरि के नाम की महिमा ऊच
नानक नामि उधरे पतित बहु मूच ।
Man Har(i) ke Nam ki mehma uch.
Nanak Nam(i) udhre patit bahu much.

चारि पदारथ जे को मागै
साध जना की सेवा लागै ।
Char(i) padarath je ko magai.
Sadh jana ke seva lagai.

जे को आपुना दूखु मिटावै
हरि हरि नामु रिदै सद गावै ।
Je ko apuna dukh(u) mitavai.
Har(i) Har(i) Nam(u) ridai sad gavai.

जे को अपुनी सोभा लोरै
साधसंगि इह हउमै छोरै ।
Je ko apuni sobha lorai.
Sadh sang(i) eh haumai chhorai.

जे को जनम मरण ते डरै
साध जना की सरनी परै ।
Je ko janam maran te darai.
Sadh jana ki sarni parai.

Great is the glory of God
who has uplifted
many a fallen one
chanting His Name !

If you wish to be granted
the four bounties of God,
look for holy saints
and serve them well !

If you wish to overcome
your sorrows and pain,
keep chanting *"Hari, Hari"*,
God's sweetest Name !

If you wish to gain
honour and glory,
giving up ego, sit
at holy men's feet !

If you are afraid
of Life and Death,
take shelter in company
of saints !

आपस कउ जो जाणै नीचा
सोऊ गनीऐ सभ ते ऊचा ।

Apas kau jo janai nicha.
Sou ganiai sabh te ucha.

निरधन कउ धनु तेरो नाउ
निथावे कउ नाउ तेरा थाउ ।

Nirdhan kau dhan(u) tero Nao.
Nithave kau Nao tera thao.

निमाने कउ प्रभ तेरो मानु
सगल घटा कउ देवहु दानु ।

Nimane kau Prabh tero man(u).
Sagal ghata kau devoh dan(u).

सरब धरम महि स्रेसट धरमु
हरि को नामु जपि निरमल करमु ।

Sarab dharma maih sresat dharma(u).
Har(i) ko Nam(u) jap(i) nirmal karam(u).

सगल क्रिआ महि ऊतम किरिआ
साधसंगि दुरमति मलु हिरिआ ।

Sagal kria maih utam kiria.
Sadh sang(i) durmat(i) mal(u) hiria.

He, who regards himself
as the lowliest of the low,
is truly the highest
of the high !

Your Name, O Merciful Lord,
is the wealth of the poor
and the shelter
of the shelterless !

From You, O Giver of charities,
honourless men
are blessed with honour
of Your Name !

Of all the religions,
the highest is to chant
the Name of God
which purifies all !

Of all the noble deeds,
the best is to cleanse your mind
under the guidance
of the holy saints !

सगल उदम महि उदमु भला
हरि का नामु जपहु जीअ सदा ।
Sagal udam maih udam (u) bhala.
Har (i) ka Nam (u) japoh jia sada.

सगल बानी महि अंम्रित बानी
हरि को जसु सुनि रसन बखानी ।
Sagal bani maih anmrit bani.
Har(i) ko jas(u) sun(i) rasan bakhani.

सगल थान ते ओहु ऊतम थानु
नानक जिह घटि बसै हरि नामु ।
Sagal than te oh (u) utam than (u).
Nanak jih ghat (i) vasai Har (i) Nam (u).

जिह प्रसादि धर ऊपरि सुखि बसहि
सुत भ्रात मीत बनिता संगि हसहि ।
Jih Prasad (i) dhar upar (i) sukh (i) baseh.
Sut bhrat mit banita sang (i) haseh.

जिह प्रसादि पीवहि सीतल जला
सुखदाई पवनु पावकु अमुला ।
Jih prasad (i) piveh sital jala.
Sukhdai pavan (u) pavak (u) amula.

Of all the efforts,
the best is to remember God
and keep chanting
His Name !

Of all the speeches,
the best is the utterance
of nectar-like
Name of God !

Of all the holy places,
the holiest is the heart
where God Himself
loves to dwell !

Through whose Grace you live
on this earth enjoying the company
of loved ones — the son, the brother,
the wife and friends... !

Through whose Grace you drink
cold water, inhale fresh air
and use fire
for your survival ... !

दीने हसत पाव करन नेत्र रसना
तिसहि तिआगि अवर संगि रचना ।
Dine hasat pav karan netr rasna.
Tiseh tiag (i) avar sang(i) rachna.

आदि अंति जो राखनहारु
तिस सिउ प्रीति न करै गवारु ।
Ad (i) ant (i) jo rakhanhar (u)
Tis sio prit (i) na karai gavar (u).

जा की सेवा नव निधि पावै
ता सिउ मूड़ा मनु नहीं लावै ।
Ja ki seva nav nidh (i) pavai.
Ta sio mura man (u) nahi lavai.

जो ठाकुरु सद सदा हजूरे
ता कउ अंधा जानत दूरे ।
Jo Thakur (u) sad sada hajure.
Ta kau andha janat dure.

जा की टहल पावै दरगह मानु
तिसहि बिसारि मुगधु अजानु ।
Ja ki tahal pavai dargah man(u).
Tiseh bisarai mugadh (u) ajan(u).

Through whose Grace you are given
these hands, feet, ears, eyes and tongue,
how come deserting such God
you start running after others ?

And it's a pity, O ignorant one,
God, who protects you
from birth till death,
is not the object of your love !

It's sad, O stupid one,
your mind is not fixed
on the One who has given you
His nine precious treasures !

How come, O blind one,
you think of God as 'distant'
though He is with you
being present everywhere !

How come, O foolish one,
you forget the One,
who gives you honour
in his court !

रतनु तिआगि कउडी संगि रचै
साचु छोडि झूठ संगि मचै ।
Ratan(u) tiag (i) kaudi sang (i) rachai.
Sach(u) chhod (i) jhuth sang (i) machai.

जो छडना सु असथिरु करि मानै
जो होवनु सो दूरि परानै ।
Jo chhadna su asthir(u) kar(i) manai.
Jo hovan(u) so dur (i) paranai.

छोडि जाइ तिस का स्रमु करै
संगि सहाई तिसु परहरै ।
Chhod (i) jae tis ka sram(u) karai.
Sang (i) sahai tis(u) par-harai.

करतूति पसू की मानस जाति
लोक पचारा करै दिनु राति ।
Kartut (i) pasu ki manas jat (i).
Lok pachara karai din(u) rat (i).

बाहरि भेख अंतरि मलु माइआ
छपसि नाहि कछु करै छपाइआ ।
Bahar (i) bhekh antar (i) mal(u) maia.
Chhapas (i) nah (i) kachh(u) karai chhapaia.

How is it, O senseless one,
ignoring the precious jewels,
you are lured by mere shells
preferring untruth to Truth !

You consider that to be lasting
which is to be left behind,
and think that to be far
which is so imminent !

You work ceaselessly for that
which is not to go with you,
but part company of the One
who is so near and dear !

Though in human garb,
you act like animals
keeping busy in publicity
and self-display !

The dress you wear is clean
but your inside is unclean,
verily you can not hide
your true self from God !

बाहरि गिआन धिआन इसनान
अंतरि बिआपै लोभु सुआनु ।
Bahar (i) gian dhian isnan.
Antar (i) biapai lobh(u) suan (u).

अंतरि अगनि बाहरि तनु सुआह
गलि पाथर कैसे तरै अथाह ।
Antar (i) agan (i) bahar (i) tan (u) suah.
Gal (i) pathar kaise tarai athah.

संगि सहाई सु आवै न चीति
जो बैराई ता सिउ प्रीति ।
Sang (i) sahai su avai na chit (i).
Jo bairai ta sio prit (i).

बलूआ के ग्रिह भीतरि बसै
अनद केल माइआ रंगि रसै ।
Balua ke graih bhitar(i) basai.
Anad kel maia rang(i) rasai.

द्रिडु करि मानै मनहि प्रतीति
कालु न आवै मूडे चीति ।
Drir (u) kar (i) mania maneh pratit (i).
Kal (u) na avai mure chit (i).

You appear to be knowledgeable,
pious, clean and a man of meditation,
but inside you dwells Greed
which is akin to a mongrel !

Inside you burns the fire of desires
but outside you apply ashes;
how, with a stone around your neck,
can you cross this ocean of life ?

You allow not your well-wishers
to enter your heart,
but befriend those
who are your enemies !

Living in the house of sand,
you play into the Mammon's hands
who leads you to the path
of self-destruction !

Willfully entertaining
illusions and delusions,
you, the ignorant one,
never think of Death !

बैर बिरोध काम क्रोध मोह

झूठ बिकार महा लोभ ध्रोह ।

Bair birodh kam krodh moh.

Jhuth bikar maha lobh dhroh.

इआहू जुगति बिहाने कई जनम

नानक राखि लेहु आपन करि करम ।

Iahu jugat (i) bihane kai janam.

Nanak rakh (i) leh (u) apan kar (i) karam.

तू ठाकुरु तुम पहि अरदासि

जीउ पिंडु सभु तेरी रासि ।

Tu Thakur (u) tum paih ardas (i)

Jio pind (u) sabh (u) teri ras (i).

तुम मात पिता हम बारिक तेरे

तुमरी क्रिपा महि सूख घनेरे ।

Tum mat pita ham barik tere.

Tumri kripa maih sukh ghanere.

दस बसतू ले पाछै पावै

एक बसतु कारनि बिखोरि गवावै ।

Das bastu le pachhai pavai.

Ek basat(u) karan(i) bikhot(i) gavavai.

Swayed by passions of hatred,
lust, anger, attachment, falsehood,
greed, betrayals and vices
of the same hue . . .

Have we passed many lives;
says Nanak, "Oh God, save me,
at least save me now,
through your Grace !"

You are my Master, O Lord,
it is my prayer to you,
"Save this body of mine
which is your capital !"

You are our Mother, our Father
we are your children;
countless pleasures you give
through Your Grace !

Alas, man readily forgets
ten bounties from God,
but loses faith if even
one of them is withdrawn !

एक भी न देइ दस भी हिरि लेइ
तउ मूड़ा कहु कहा करेइ ।
Ek bhi na de-e das bhi hir (i) le-e.
Tau mura kah (u) kaha kare-e.

अपुनी अमान कछु बहुरि साहु लेइ
अगिआनी मनि रोसु करेइ ।
Apuni aman kachh (u) bahur (i) sah (u) le-e.
Agiani man (i) ros(u) kare-e.

अपनी परतीति आप ही खोवै
बहुरि उस का बिस्वासु न होवै ।
Apni partit (i) ap hi khovai.
Bahur (i) us ka bisvas (u) na hovai.

जिस की बसतु तिसु आगै राखै
प्रभ की आगिआ मानै माथै ।
Jis ki basat (u) tis (u) agai rakhai.
Prabh ki agia mania mathai.

उस ते चउगुन करै निहालु
नानक साहिबु सदा दइआलु ।
Us te chaugun karai nihal (u).
Nanak sahib (u) sada dae-al (u).

But what can you do, O ignorant one,
if God withdraws
all the ten, leaving not
a single one behind ?

If perchance, He takes back
what belongs to Him,
you, the foolish one,
show anger and resentment !

And the outcome is:
you lose your credentials
ceasing to be trusted
by God any more !

But, if bowing to His Will
and following His command,
you offer to return
what is truly His . . .

"God, the Kind One," says Nanak,
overwhelms you with joy
giving four times more
He had given earlier !

अनिक भाति माइआ के हेत
सरपर होवत जानु अनेत ।
Anik bhat (i) maia ke het.
Sarpar hovat jan(u) anet.

बिरख की छाइया सिउ रंगु लावै
ओह बिनसै उहु मनि पछुतावै ।
Birkh ki chhaia sio rang (u) lavai.
Oh binsai uh (u) man (i) pachhutavai.

जो दीसै सो चालनहारु
लपटि रहिओ तह अंधु अंधारु ।
Jo disai so chalan-har (u).
Lapat (i) rahio tah andh andhar (u).

मिथिआ तनु धनु कुटंबु सबाइआ
मिथिआ हउमै ममता माइआ ।
Mithia tan (u) dhan (u) kutanb (u) sabaia.
Mithia haumai mamta maia.

मिथिआ राज जोबन धन माल
मिथिआ काम क्रोध बिकराल ।
Mithia raj joban dhan mal.
Mithia kam krodh bikral.

Wordly ties and attachments
do you no good;
with passage of time
they remain no more !

When ignoring the tree,
you fall in love with its shadow,
you are bound to repent
in the end !

All that you see is short-lived
and will pass away;
but the blind self continues
to cling to the ephemeral !

False are your body,
wealth and family;
false are attachments,
ego and illusions !

False are your power,
youth and wealth;
false are lust, anger
and untruth !

मिथिआ ध्रोह मोह अभिमानु
मिथिआ आपस ऊपरि करत गुमानु ।
Mithia dhroh moh abhiman (u).
Mithia apas upar (i) karat guman (u).

बिनु बूझे मिथिआ सभ भए
सफल देह नानक हरि हरि नाम लए ।
Bin (u) bujhe mithia sabh bhae.
Saphal deh Nanak Har (i) Har (i) Nam lae.

बिनु सिमरन दिनु रैनि ब्रिथा बिहाइ
मेघ बिना जिउ खेती जाइ ।
Bin (u) simran din (u) rain (i) britha bihae.
Megh bina jio kheti jae.

गोबिद भजन बिनु ब्रिथे सभ काम
जिउ किरपन के निरारथ दाम ।
Gobid bhajan bin (u) brithe sabh kam.
Jio kirpan ke nirarath dam.

धंनि धंनि ते जन जिह घटि बसिओ हरि नाउ
नानक ता कै बलि बलि जाउ ।
Dhann (i) dhann (i) te jan jih ghat (i) basio Har (i) Nau.
Nanak ta kai bal (i) bal (i) jau.

False are betrayals,
clingings and self-love;
false is pride
in yourself !

Without Divine knowledge,
everything is false;
life dedicated to God
alone is true !

As the crop is useless
without rain-bearing clouds,
so are the day and night
without God's Name !

All endeavours, without
His Name, are useless
like the wealth
of a miserly man !

Blessed are those in whose heart
God resides;
says Nanak, "I admire
such noble souls !"

रहत अवर कछु अवर कमावत
मनि नही प्रीति मुखहु गंढ लावत ।

Rahat avar kachh (u) avar kamavat.
Man (i) nahi prit (i) mukhoh gandh lavat.

जाननहार प्रभू परबीन
बाहरि भेख न काहू भीन ।

Janan-har Prabhu parbin.
Bahr (i) bhekh na kahu bhin.

अवर उपदेसै आपि न करै
आवत जांवत जनमै मरै ।

Avar updesai ap (i) ne karai.
Avat javat janmai marai.

उपाव सिआनप सगल ते रहत
सभु कछु जानै आतम की रहत ।

Upav sianap sagal te rahat.
Sabh (u) kachh (u) janai atam ki rahat.

जिसु भावै तिसु लए लड़ि लाइ
थान थनतरि रहिआ समाइ ।

Jis (u) bhavai tis (u) lae lar (i) lae.
Than thanantar (i) rahia samae.

You do one thing but profess another,
your love for God is not true;
but through your sweet tongue,
you lure others to yourself!

But God, the Wise One,
knows everything
and is not impressed
by your looks!

What you preach to others
you seldom do,
and so, fated are you,
for another cycle of Life and Death!

Though free from wiles and guiles,
God knows what goes on
within your mind and heart
and cannot be cheated!

Love for him sprouts
only in one, liked by God;
present is He everywhere
and in everything, seen, unseen!

साध के संगि अगोचरु मिलै
साध कै संगि सदा परफुलै ।

Sadh kai sang (i) agochar (u) milai.
Sadh kai sang (i) sada parphulai.

साध कै संगि न कतहूं धावै
साधसंगि असथिति मनु पावै ।

Sadh kai sang (i) na kat-hun dhavai.
Sadh sang (i) asthit (i) man (u) pavai.

साधसंगि दुसमन सभि मीत
साधू कै संगि महा पुनीत ।

Sadh sang (i) dusman sabh (i) mit.
Sadhu kai sang (i) maha punit.

साध कै संगि नाही को मंदा
साधसंगि जाने परमानंदा ।

Sadh kai sang (i) nahi ko manda.
Sadh sang (i) jane parma-nanda.

साध कै संगि नाही हउ तापु
साध कै संगि तजै सभु आपु ।

Sadh kai sang (i) nahi hau tap (u).
Sadh kai sang (i) tajai sabh (u) ap (u).

You can see the unseen God
through the company of saints
and always stay
in the blissful state !

In the company of saints,
your mind stops to waiver
being stabilised and fixed
on God for ever !

Your enemies turn into friends
in the company of saints
and your life becomes
absolutely pure !

No evil befalls you
in the company of saints
and you gain knowledge
of the Supreme !

In the company of saints,
you are not gripped
by the fever of ego
which recedes on its own !

साध कै संगि द्रिड़ै सभि धरम
साध कै संगि केवल पारब्रहम ।
Sadh kai sang (i) drirai sabh (i) dharam.
Sadh kai sang (i) keval Parbrahm.

ब्रहम गिआनी सदा निरलेप
जैसे जल महि कमल अलेप ।
Brahm-giani sada nir-lep.
Jaise jal maih kamal alep.

ब्रहम गिआनी निरमल ते निरमला
जैसे मैलु न लागै जला ।
Brahm-giani nirmal te nirmala.
Jaise mail (u) na lagai jala.

ब्रहम गिआनी सदा समदरसी
ब्रहम गिआनी की द्रिसटि अंम्रित बरसी ।
Brahm-giani sada sam-darsi.
Brahm-giani ki drist (i) anmrit (u) barsi.

ब्रहम गिआनी बंधन ते मुकता
ब्रहम गिआनी की निरमल जुगता ।
Brahm-giani bandhan te mukta
Brahm-giani ki nirmal jugta.

His faith is strengthened
in God and religion
and he is with God
and God alone !

Brahmagyani (the knower of God)
is like a lotus, which though
in water, remains
untouched !

Brahmagyani, the purest of the pure,
is like water
unpolluted
by filth !

Brahmagyani is same to all,
His eyes, full of love,
showering nectar
on all alike !

Pure and noble, Brahmagyani
has no personal bonds;
his life being based
on reason and discipline !

ब्रहम गिआनी एक ऊपरि आस
ब्रहम गिआनी का नही बिनास ।

Brahm-giani ek upar(i) as.
Brahm-giani ka nahi binas.

प्रभु की आगिआ आतम हितावै
जीवन मुकति सोऊ कहावै ।

Prabh ki agia atam hitavai.
Jivan mukat(i) sou kahavai.

तैसा हरखु तैसा उसु सोगु
सदा अनंदु तह नहीं बिओगु ।

Taisa harakh(u) taisa us(u) sog(u).
Sada anand(u) tah nahi biog(u).

तैसा सुवरनु तैसी उसु माटी
तैसा अंम्रितु तैसी बिखु खाटी ।

Taisa suvaran(u) taisi us(u) mati.
Taisa anmrit(u) taisi bikh(u) khati.

तैसा मानु तैसा अभिमानु
तैसा रंकु तैसा राजानु ।

Taisa man(u) taisa abhiman(u).
Taisa rank(u) taisa rajan(u).

Brahmagyani pins his faith
on One God
and shall never
be destroyed !

Jeevanmukta, a liberated one,
is he, who follows
God's commands
with devotion and love !

Equal to happiness and sorrow
and contended for ever,
he knows not the pangs
of separation !

To him gold and clay
are the same,
and so are the nectar
and the poison !

Alike to him are praise and blame,
no distinction he makes
between the pauper
and the king !

प्रभ भावै मानुख गति पावै।
प्रभ भावै ता पाथर तरावै।।
Prabh bhavai manukh gat(i) pavai.
Prabh bhavai ta pathar travai.

प्रभ भावै बिनु सास ते राखै।
प्रभ भावै ता हरि गुण भाखै।।
Prabh bhavai bin(u) sas te rakhai.
Prabh bhavai ta Har(i) gun bhakahi.

प्रभ भावै ता पतित उधारै।
आपि करै आपन बीचारै।।
Prabh bhavai ta patit udharai.
Ap(i) karai apan bicharai.

जो भावै सो कार करावै।
नानक द्रिसटी अवरू न आवै।।
Jo bhavai so kar karavai.
Nanak dristi avar(u) na avai.

इस कै हाथि होइ ता सभु किछु लेई।
जो तिसु भावै सोई करेइ।।
Is kai hath(i) hoe ta sabh(u) kichh(u) le-e.
Jo tis(u) bhavai soi kare-e.

On God's Will depends
man's salvation;
He can even make
a stone swim!

If God wills, a man
can live without breath;
through His Grace alone
one sings His glory!

If God wills, He can
uplift the fallen;
He always thinks and acts
on His own!

What God wills
is done;
"No one is like him,"
says Nanak !

Man would grab all
if he could;
but no, only that prevails
which God wills !

अनजानत बिखिआ महि रचै।
ते ज़ानत आपन आप बचै।।
An-janat bikhia maih rachai.
Je janat apan ap bachai.

जिस कै अंतरि राज अभिमानु
सो नरकपाती होवत सुआनु ।
Jis kai antar(i) raj abhiman(u).
So narak pati hovat suan(u).

जो जानै मै जोबनवंतु
सो होवत बिसटा का जंतु ।
Jo janai mai joban-vant(u).
So hovat bista ka jant(u).

आपस कउ करमवंतु कहावै
जनमि मरै बहु जोनि भ्रमावै ।
Apas kau karam-vant(u) kahavai.
Janam(i) marai bahu jon(i) bhramavai.

धन भूमि का जो करै गुमानु
सो मूरखु अंधा अगिआनु ।
Dhan bhum(i) ka jo karai guman(u).
So murakh(u) andha agian(u).

In ignorance man indulges
in sensual pleasures,
if, aware of outcome,
he could save his soul !

Man, who is proud
of his power
is like a dog
living in the hell !

Man, who is proud
of his youth,
is like an insect
of the worst breed !

Man, who is proud
of his fortune,
will ever wander
through life and death !

Man, who is proud
of his land and wealth,
is ignorant, blind,
lacking in knowledge !

धनवंता होइ करि गरबावै ।
त्रिण समानि कछु संगि न जावै ।।
Dhanvanta hoe kar(i) garbavai.
Trin saman(i) Kachh(u) sang(i) na javai.

बहु लसकर मानुख ऊपरि करे आस ।
पल भीतरि ता का होइ बिनास ।।
Bahu lascar manukh upar(i) kare as.
Pal bhitar(i) ta ka hoe binas.

सभ ते आप जानै बलवंतु ।
खिन महि होइ जाइ भसमंतु ।।
Sabh te ap janai balvant(u).
Khin maih hoe jae bhasmant(u).

किसै न बदै आपि अहंकारी ।
धरम राइ तिसु करे खुआरी ।।
Kisai na badai ap(i) ahankari.
Dharam-rae tis(u) kare khuari.

कोटि करम करै हउ धारे ।
स्रमु पावै सगले बिरथारे ।।
Kot(i) karam karai hau dhare.
Sram(u) pavai sagle birthare.

Let a man, proud of his riches,
know, that not a straw
will go with him
after his death!

He, who prides himself
on army and men,
is destroyed
in the blinking of an eye!

He, who thinks he is
the strongest of all,
is reduced to ashes
in a moment's time!

Man, who out of his ego,
disregards others, giving
no recognition to them,
is punished by the Divine Judge!

Even if an egoist performs
millions of noble acts,
they all go waste; he gets
only misery in return!

अनिक जतन करे आतम नही द्रवै ।
हरि दरगह कहु कैसे गवै ।।
Anik jatan kar(i) atam nahi dravai.
Har(i) dargah kahu kaise gavai.

आपस कउ जो भला कहावै ।
तिसहि भलाई निकटि न आवै ।।
Apas kau jo bhala kahavai.
Tiseh bhalai nikat(i) na avai.

जब लगु जानै मुझ ते कछु होइ ।
तब इस कउ सुखु ना ही कोइ ।।
Jab lag(u) janai mujh te kachh(u) hoe.
Tab is kau sukh (u) nahi koe.

जब इह जानै मैं किछु करता ।
तब लग गरभ जोनि महि फिरता ।।
Jab eh janai mai kichh(u) karta.
Tab lag(u) garabh jon(i) maih phirta.

जब धारै कोऊ बैरी मीतु ।
तब लगु निहचलु नाही चीतु ।।
Jab dharai kou bairi mit(u).
Tab lag(u) nihchal(u) nahi chit(u).

How can a man
with his heart
unsoftened, ever enter
God's venerable court?

Man, who calls himself
good and pious,
is not even close
to what is goodness!

So long as he thinks
"I" can do something,
he is bound to fail
to find happiness!

So long as he thinks
"I am the doer",
condemned he will be
to birth and rebirth!

So long as he has
enemies or friends,
his mind cannot enjoy
the perfect peace!

जब लगु मोह मगन संगि माइ।
तब लगु धरम राइ देइ सजाइ।।
Jab lag(u) moh magan sang(i) mae.
Tab lag(u) Dharam-rae de-e sajae.

प्रभ किरपा ते बंधन तूटै।
गुरप्रसादि नानक हउ छूटै।।
Prabh kirpa te bandhan tutai.
Gur Prasad(i) Nanak hau chhutai.

सहस खटे लख कउ उठि धावै।
त्रिपति न आवै माइआ पाछै पावै।।
Sahas khate lakh kau uth(i) dhavai.
Tripat(i) na avai maia pachhai pavai.

अनिक भोग बिखिआ के करै।
नह त्रिपतावै खपि खपि मरै।।
Anik bhog bikhia ke karai.
Nah triptavai khap(i) khap(i) marai.

बिना संतोख नही कोऊ राजै।
सुपन मनोरथ ब्रिथे सभ काजै।।
Bina santokh nahi kou rajai.
Supan manorath brithe sabh kajai.

So long as man is attached
to the objects of pleasure,
he continues to get
punishment from God!

It is through grace
of God and the guru,
a man is freed from
wordly bonds and ego!

After acquiring thousands,
man aspires after lakhs,
but running after the Mammon
gives him no fulfillment!

Despite his indulgence
and wrong doings,
he is never satisfied, dying
many a time before his death!

Unless content,
he cannot feel fulfilled;
his efforts go waste
like the wishful dreams!

नाम रंगि सरब सुखु होइ।
बडभागी किसै परापति होइ।।
Nam rang(i) sarab sukh(u) hoe.
Bad-bhagi kisai parapat(i) hoe.

करन करावन करनैहारू।
इस कै हाथि कहा बीचारू।।
Karan caravan karnai-har(u).
Is kai hat(i) kaha bichar(u).

जो किछु कीनो सु अपनै रंगि।
सभ ते दूरि सभहू कै संगि।।
Jo kichh(u) kino su apnai rang(i).
Sabh te dur(i) sabh-hu kai sang(i).

बूझै देखै करै बिबेक।
आपहि एक आपहि अनेक।।
Bujhai dekhai karai bibek.
Apeh ek apeh anek.

मरै न बिनसै आवै न जाइ।
नानक सद ही रहिआ समाइ।।
Marai ne binsai avai na jae.
Nanak sad hi rahia samae.

Blessed is he, who has found
contentment in his heart
and enjoys real happiness
in God's Name!

God is the Doer of everything
and through Him things are done;
poor self having
nothing in his hands!

Whatever He has done
(or He does)
is out of His sweet will;
He is distant and yet so near!

He has His own reason
and logic for everything;
though One, He assumes
many forms!

Neither is He born nor dead
nor can he be ever destroyed;
ever present is He
in everything!

सति सति सति प्रभु सुआमी।
गुरपरसादि किनै वखिआनी।।

Sat(i) sat(i) sat(i) Prabh(u) suami.
Gur parsad(i) kinai vakhiani.

सचु सचु सचु सभु कीना।
कोटि मधे किनै बिरलै चीना।।

Sach(u) sach(u) sach(u) sabh(u) kina.
Kot(i) madhe kinai birlai china.

भला भला भला तेरा रूप।
अति सुंदर अपार अनूप।।

Bhala bhala bhala tera rup.
At(i) sundar apar anup.

निरमल निरमल निरमल तेरी बाणी।
घटि घटि सुनी स्रवन बख्याणी।।

Nirmal nirmal nirmal teri bani.
Ghat(i) ghat(i) suni sravan bakhyani.

पवित्र पवित्र पवित्र पुनीत।
नामु जपै नानक मनि प्रीति।।

Pavitr pavitr pavitr punit.
Nam(u) japai Nanak man(i) prit(i).

Real, real, real is His Name
— this is the secret revealed
by one, blessed
with guru's grace!

Real, real, real is everything
created by God;
though one in a million
knows this truth!

Splendid, splendid, splendid is
God's form, and verily
He is most Glorious,
Limitless and Unparallaled!

Sacred, sacred, sacred is
His Word, which gives
immense peace
when uttered or heard!

Pure, pure, pure is God,
says Nanak, and one
who repeats His Name, with mind
fixed on Him, will be sanctified!

संत का निंदकु महा अतताई ।
संत का निंदकु खिनु टिकनु न पाई ।।

Sant ka nindak(u) maha at-tai.
Sant ka nindak(u) khin(u) tikan(u) na pai.

संत का निंदकु महा हतिआरा ।
संत का निंदकु परमेसुरि मारा ।।

Sant ka nindak(u) maha hatiara.
Sant ka nindak(u) Parmesur(i) mara.

संत के निंदक कउ सरब रोग ।
संत के निंदक कउ बिजोग ।।

Sant ke nindak kau sarab rog.
Sant ke nindak kau sada bijog.

संत का दोखी महा अहंकारी ।
संत का दोखी सदा बिकारी ।।

Sant ka dokhi maha ahankari.
Sant ka dokhi sada bikari.

संत का दोखी अध बीच ते टूटै ।
संत का दोखी कितै काजि न पहूचै ।।

Sant ka dokhi adh bich te tutai.
Sant ka dokhi kitai kaj(i) na pahuchai.

Man, speaking ill of saints,
and finding fault with them,
is a sinner and will find
no shelter anywhere!

He is an odious assassin
living under God's wrath,
and will be shattered
by His punishment!

A victim of all ailments,
he will be subjected
to continuous separation
by the justice of God!

Not only full
of ego is he,
but also tainted
by many a vice!

Bent and broken
from the middle,
he is unable to accomplish
any goal!

संत का दोखी अंतर ते थोथा।
जिउ सास बिना मिरतक की लोथा ।।
Sant ka dokhi antar te thotha.
Jio sas bina mirtak ki lotha.

संत का दोखी इउ बिललाइ ।
जिउ जल बिहून मछुली तड़फड़ाइ ।।
Sant ka dokhi eo bil-lae.
Jio jal bihun machhuli tarpharae.

संत का दोखी सदा सहकाईऐ ।
संत का दोखी न मरै न जीवाईऐ ।।
Sant ka dokhi sada sahkaiai.
Sant ka dokhi na marai na jivaiai.

मानुख की टेक ब्रिथी सभ जानु।
देवन कउ एकै भगवानु ।।
Manukh ki tek brithi sabh jan(u).
Devan kau ekai bhagvan(u).

मारै राखै एको आपि ।
मानुख कै किछु नाही हाथि ।।
Marai rakhai eko ap(i).
Manukh kai kichh(u) nahi hath(i)

Being hollow within,
he is like the body
of the one, who has
ceased to breathe !

Restless like a fish
out of water,
there is no end
to his miseries !

Like an ever thirsty
man is he,
who neither dies
nor truly lives !

Useless it is to rely
on anyone's support;
it's God (not man !)
who gives us all !

It is for God alone to kill
or to protect;
helpless is man, nothing is
in his control !

टूटी गाढनहार गोपाल ।
सरब जीआ आपे प्रतिपाल ।।
Tuti gadhan-har Gopal.
Sarab jia ape pratipal.

सगल की चिंता जिसु मन माहि ।
तिस ते बिरथा कोई नाही ।।
Sagal ki chinta jis(u) man mah(i).
Tis te birtha koi nah(i).

तिस बिनु नाही तेरै किछु काम।
गति नानक जपि एक हरि नाम ।।
Tis(u) bin(u) nahi terai kichh(u) kam.
Gat(i) Nanak jap(i) ek Har(i) Nam.

रूपवंतु होइ नाही मोहै।
प्रभु की जोति सगल घट सोहै।।
Rup-vant(u) hoe nahi mohai.
Prabh ki jot(i) sagal ghat sohai.

धनवंता होइ किआ को गरबै।
जा सभु किछु तिस का दीआ दरबै।।
Dhan-vanta hoe kia ko garbai.
Ja sabh(u) kichh(u) tis ka dia darbai.

Broken hearts, the Lord mends,
He is the Protector
of all beings
on this earth !

Concerned is God for every body;
no one approaching Him
has ever returned
empty handed !

Nothing is accomplished
without God,
"So, "says Nanak, "Keep Chanting
Hari, Hari, His Name !"

God is not charmed
by one's looks;
It is His light itself
which shines through all !

If one is rich,
so what ?
all his wealth has come
from Him alone !

अति सूरा जे कोऊ कहावै।
प्रभ की कला बिना कह धावै।।
At(i) sura je kou kahavai.
Prabh ki kala bina kah dhavai.

जे को होइ बहै दातारू।
तिसु देनहारू जानै गावारू।।
Je ko hoe bahai datar(u).
Tis(u) Den-har(u) janai gavar(u).

जिउ मंदर कउ थामै थंमनु।
तिउ गुर का सबदु मनहि असथंमनु।।
Jio mandar kau thamai thanman(u).
Tio gur ka sabad(u) maneh asthanman(u).

जिउ पाखाणु नाव चड़ि तरै।
प्राणी गुर चरण लगतु निसतरै।।
Jio pakhan(u) nav char(i) tarai.
Prani gur charan lagat(u) nis-tarai.

जिउ अंधकार दीपक परगासु।
गुर दरसनु देखि मनि होइ बिगासु।।
Jio andhkar dipak pargas(u).
Gur darsan(u) dekh(i) man(i) hoe bigas(u).

If some one is called brave,
from whom, except God,
has he acquired
this valour ?

He, who is called a man
of great charity,
remember, it is God
not he, who is the Giver !

As the pillars support
a house's roofs,
so is devotee's mind
through Guru's grace !

As a stone crosses
a river on a boat,
so does a devotee traverse
life's ocean through guru's grace !

As the earthen lamp
dispels darkness,
and lights up the world,
so does Guru's sight !

जिउ महा उदिआन महि मारगु पावै।
तिउ साधू संगि मिलि जोति प्रगटावै।।
Jio maha udian maih marag(u) pavai.
Tio sadhu sang(i) mil(i) jot(i) pragtavai.

मन मूरख काहे बिललाईऐ ।
पुरब लिखे का लिखिआ पाईऐ ।।
Man murakh kahe bil-laiai.
Purab likhe ka likhia paiai.

दूख सूख प्रभ देवनहारु।
अवर तिआगि तू तिसहि चितारु ।।
Dukh sukh Prabh devan-har(u).
Avar tiag(i) tu tiseh chitar(u).

कउन बसतु आई तेरै संग।
लपटि रहिओ रसि लोभी पतंग।।
Kaun basat(u) ai terai sang.
Lapat(i) rahio ras(i) lobhi patang.

राम नाम जपि हिरदे माहि।
नानक प्रति सेती धरि जाहि।।
Ram Nam jap(i) hirde mah(i)
Nanak pat(i) seti ghar(i) jah(i).

The wisdom of saints
illumines the mind
just as one comes upon
a path in wilderness!

Why this hue and cry
O, ignorant self,
your suffering stems
from your own doings !

Giver of joy and sorrow
is God and God alone;
leaving all others
just chant His Name !

What did you bring
at the time of birth?
why then keep clinging to
wordly objects like a moth?

"Repeating God's Name
in your heart,
go back honourably from
whence you came," says Nanak.

साध सेवा वडभागी पाईऐ ।
साधसंगि हरि कीरतनु गाईऐ ।।
Sadh seva vad-bhagi paiai.
Sadh sang(i) Har(i) kirtan(u) gaiai.

अनिक बिघन ते साधू राखै ।
हरि गुन गाइ अंम्रित रसु चाखै ।।
Anik bighan te sadhu rakhai.
Har(i) Gun gae anmrit ras(u) chakhai.

मिरतक कउ जीवालनहार ।
भूखे कउ देवत अधार ।।
Mirtak kau jivalan-har.
Bhukhe kau devat adhar.

सभु किछु तिस का ओहु करनै जोगु ।
तिसु बिनु दूसर होआ न होगु ।।
Sabh(u) kichh(u) tis ka oh(u) karnai-jog(u).
Tis(u) bin(u) dusar hoa na hog(u).

हरन भरन जा का नेत्र फोरु ।
तिस का मंत्रु न जानै होरु ।।
Haran bharan ja ka netr phor(u).
Tis ka mantr(u) na janai hor(u).

Only a lucky few
get a chance to serve
the guru — sing, sing God's
glory in his company!

Such a guru, drinking
the nectar of God's Name,
keeps you safe
from all obstacles!

God, the Almighty,
restores life to the dead;
He feeds and supports
the hungry and the needy!

To God, belongs everything,
He alone accomplishes all;
no one has ever been
or will be like Him!

In the twinkling of an eye
God can create or destroy;
no one can know
what is in His mind!

नाम के धारे सगले जंत।
नाम के धारे खंड ब्रहमंड।।
Nam ke dhare sagle jant.
Nam ke dhare khand brahmand.

नाम के धारे सिम्रिति बेद पुरान।
नाम के धारे सुनन गिआन धिआन।।
Nam ke dhare Simrit(i) Bed Puran.
Nam ke dhare sunan gian dhian.

नाम के धारे आगास पाताल।
नाम के धारे सगल आकार।।
Nam ke dhare agas patal.
Nam ke dhare sagal akar.

रूपु सति जा का सति असथानु।
पुरखु सति केवल परधानु।।
Rup(u) sat(i) ja ka sat(i) asthan(u).
Purakh(u) sat(i) keval pardhan(u).

करतूति सति सति जा की बाणी।
सति पुरख सभ माहि समाणी।।
Kartut(i) sat(i) sat(i) ja ki Bani.
Sat(i) purakh sabh mah(i) samani.

Supported by God's Name
are all creatures,
all regions
and all worlds...

And so are all
Smritis, Vedas and Puranas,
the Divine knowledge
and all forms of meditation!

Dependent on God's Name
are firmaments, nether region
and all heavenly bodies
of different kinds!

True is His form
and true His place;
the Truthful God
is the Lord of all!

True are His acts
and true His words;
the Truthful God
is present everywhere !

सति करमु जा की रचना सति ।
मूलु सति सति उतपति ।।
Sat(i) karam(u) ja ki rachna sat(i).
Mul(u) sat(i) sat(i) utpat(i).

ठाकुर का सेवकु आगिआकारी ।
ठाकुर का सेवकु सदा पूजारी ।।
Thakur ka sevak(u) agia-kari.
Thakur ka sevak(u) sada pujari.

ठाकुर के सेवक कै मनि परतीति ।
ठाकुर के सेवक की निरमल रीति ।।
Thakur ke sevak kai man(i) partit(i).
Thakur ke sevak ki nirmal rit(i).

ठाकुर कउ सेवकु जानै संगि ।
प्रभ का सेवकु नाम कै रंगि ।।
Thakur kau sevak(u) janai sang(i).
Prabh ka sevak(u) Nam kai rang(i).

सेवक कउ प्रभ पालनहारा ।
सेवक की राखै निरंकारा ।।
Sevak kau Prabh Palan-hara.
Sevak ki rakhai Nirankara.

True are His deeds
and true His Creation;
the Truthful God's
origin is also true !

The true servant of God
follows His commands,
constantly worshipping
and chanting His Name !

God's true servant
is full of faith
and his actions
are absolutely pure !

Being fully aware
of God's presence,
He is immersed
in His Name !

Shielded is His servent
from all harms;
his honour is protected
by His own arms !

अपुने जन का परदा ढाकै ।
अपने सेवक की सरपर राखै ।।
Apune jan ka parda dhakai.
Apne sevak ki sarpar rakhai.

नीकी कीरी महि कल राखै ।
भसम करै लसकर कोटि लाखै ।।
Niki kiri maih kal rakhai.
Bhasam karai laskar kot(i) lakhai.

जिस का सासु न काढत आपि ।
ता कउ राखत दे करि हाथ ।।
Jis ka sas(u) na kadhat ap(i).
Ta kau rakhat de kar(i) hath.

मानस जतन करत बहु भाति ।
तिस के करतब बिरथे जाति ।।
Manas jatan karat bahu bhat(i).
Tis ke kartab birthe jat(i).

काहे सोच करहि रे प्राणी ।
जपि नानक प्रभ अलख विडाणी ।।
Kahe soch kareh re prani.
Jap(i) Nanak Prabh Alakh vidani.

God puts a lid on
devotee's flaws,
blessing and saving him
from a bad name !

If God empowers
even a small ant,
it can destroy
an army of millions!

If God does not will
one to cease breathing,
He protects him
by extending His hand!

Many efforts a man may make
but they are all
brought to nought
if God is not willing !

"Why worry, "O man,"
says Nanak, "All you need
is to chant
God's Name !"

बारं बार बार प्रभु जपीऐ।
पी अंम्रितु इहु मनु तनु ध्रपीऐ।।
Baran bar bar Prabh(u) japiai.
Pi anmrit(u) eh(u) man(u) tan(u) dhrapiai.

नाम रतनु जिनि गुरमुखि पाइआ।
तिसु किछु अवरू नाही द्रिसटाइआ।।
Nam rattan(u) jin(i) gurmukh(i) paia.
Tis(u) kichh(u) avar(u) nahi dristaia.

नामु धनु नामो रूपु रंगु।
नामो सुखु हरि नाम का संगु।।
Nam(u) dhan(u) Namo rup(u) rang(u).
Namo sukh(u) Har(i) Nam ka sang(u).

नाम रसि जो जन त्रिपताने।
मन तन नामहि नामि समाने।।
Nam ras(i) jo jan triptane.
Man tan nameh Nam(i) samane.

ऊठत बैठत सोवत नाम।
कहु नानम जन कै सद काम।।
Uthat baithat sovat Nam.
Kahu Nanak jan kai sad kam.

Drink and ever drink
the nectar of God's Name;
let your mind and senses
be saturated to the full!

Man, who has found
the jewel of His Name,
sees nothing but
Him everywhere !

Name is his wealth,
Name his form and colour;
he spends all the time
repeating His Name!

Man, who satiates himself
with God's Name,
has his mind ever
fixed on Him !

Says Nanak, "Remember God
standing, sitting and sleeping;
remembering Him
is man's prime duty !"

अवरि उपाव सभि मीत बिसारहु ।
चरन कमल रिद महि उरि धारहु ।।
Avar(i) upav sabh(i) mit bisaroh.
Charan kamal rid maih ur(i) dharoh.

करन कारन सो प्रभु समरथु ।
द्रिड़ करि गहहु नामु हरि वथु ।।
Karan karan so Prabh(u) samarath(u).
Drir(u) kar(i) gahoh Nam(u) Har(i) vath(u).

इहु धनु संचहु होवहु भगवंत ।
संत जना का निरमल मंत ।।
Eh(u) dhan(u) sanchoh hovoh bhagvant.
Sant jana ka nirmal mant.

एक आस राखहु मन माहि ।
सरब रोग नानक मिटि जाहि ।।
Ek as rakhoh man mah(i).
Sarab rog Nanak mit(i) jah(i).

अनिक उपावी रोगु न जाइ ।
रोगु मिटै हरि अवखधु लाइ ।।
Anik Upavi rog(u) na jae.
Rog(u) mitai Har(i) avkhadh(u) lae.

Drop all efforts, O dear ones,
and install the Lotus Feet
of Great God
in your heart !

God, the Doer of everything,
is all-powerful;
hold fast to His Name,
hold it firm !

To become truly rich,
accumulate the wealth
of God's Name — this is
the wisdom of the wise !

" If all your hopes
are fixed on One God",
says Nanak, "All your
ailments will go !"

The illness, not remedied
despite efforts, will go
on taking the medicine
of God's Name !

एको जपि एको सालाहि।
एकु सिमरि एको मन आहि ।।
Eko jai(i) eko salah(i).
Ek(u) simar(i) eko man ah(i).

एकस के गुन गाउ अनंत ।
मनि तनि जापि एक भगवंत ।।
Ekas ke gun gao anant.
Man(i) tan(i) jap(i) ek bhagvant.

ऐको एकु एकु हरि आपि।
पूरन पूरि रहिओ प्रभु बिआपि ।।
Eko ek(u) ek(u) Har(i) ap(i).
Puran pur(i) rahio Prabh(u) biap(i).

जाचक जनु जाचै प्रभ दानु।
करि किरपा देवहु हरि नामु ।।
Jachak(u) jan(u) jachai Prabh dan(u).
Kar(i) kirpa devoh Har(i) Nam(u).

सदा सदा प्रभ के गुन गावउ।
सासि सासि प्रभ तुमहि धियावउ ।।
Sada sada Prabh ke gun gavau.
Sas(i) sas(i) Prabh tumeh dhiavau.

Chant the Holy Name
of God, who is One;
worship the One and
keep the One in your heart !

Praise the glory
of the limitless One;
Chant His Name,
He is One, and only One !

God is One, One
and only One;
He, the Perfect One,
pervades all !

I, your humble servant,
seek nothing, beg nothing
but only the pleasure
of chanting Your Name !

Let me sing and sing
Your glory for ever,
thinking of You and you alone
with every breath of mine!

एक ओट एको आधारु ।
नानकु मागै नामु प्रभ सारु ।।
Ek ot eko adhar(u).
Nanak(u) magai Nam(u) Prabh sar(u).

सो अंतरि से बाहरि अनंत ।
घटि घटि बिआपि रहिआ भगवंत ।।
So antar(i) so bahar(i) anant.
Ghat(i) ghat (i) biap(i) rahia bhagvant.

धरनि माहि आकास पइआल ।
सरब लोक पूरन प्रतिपाल ।।
Dharan(i) mah(i) akas pae-al.
Sarab lok puran pratipal.

पउण पाणी बैसंतर माहि ।
चारि कुंट दह दिसे समाहि ।।
Paun pani baisantar mah(i).
Char(i) kunt dah-dise samah(i).

तिस ते भिंन नही को ठाउ ।
गुरप्रसादि नानक सुखु पाउ ।।
Tis te bhinn nahi ko thao.
Gur Prasad(i) Nanak sukh(u) pao.

"My only Support and Refuge
are you, O Lord,"
says Nanak, "Give me the gift
of Your Name !"

Outside of everything is He
and so also inside;
the limitless One pervades
each and every atom !

Protector of the universe,
present is He everywhere;
the earth, the heavens,
the sky and the nether region ...

In wind, in water and in fire
is present He ;
permeated by Him are four
quarters and ten destinations !

"No place is without Him,"
says Nanak,
"Through your Guru's grace,
be happy forever!"

चिति चितवहु नाराइण एक।
एक रूप जा के रंग अनेक ।।
Chit(i) chivoh Narain ek.
Ek rup ja ke rang anek.

सफल जीवनु सफलु ता का संगु।
जा कै मनि लागा हरि रंगु ।।
Saphal jivan(u) saphal(u) ta ka sang(u).
Ja kai man(i) laga Har(i) rang(u).

सुखमनी सहज गोबिंद गुन नाम ।
जिसु मनि बसै सु होत निधान ।।
Sukhmani sahaj Gobind gun Nam.
Jis(u) man(i) basai so hot nidhan.

सरब इछा ता की पूरन होइ ।
प्रधान पुरखु प्रगटु सभ लोइ ।।
Sarab ichha ta ki puran hoe.
Pradhan purakh(u) pragat(u) sabh loe.

जनम मरन ता का दूखु निवारै ।
दुलभ देह ततकाल उधारै ।।
Janam maran ta ka dukh(u) nivarai.
Dulabh deh tat-kal udharai.

Keep the One God
in your heart;
His form is One
though manifestations many !

Blessed is his life
and blessed his company
whose heart is dyed
in God's Name !

He, in whose heart, Sukhmani,
treasure of God's bliss, dwells,
becomes an embodiment
of Divine Wealth !

Elevated and uplifted,
with his desires fulfilled,
he becomes the leader
of all!

Freed from the pangs
of life and death,
his birth as a human,
is fructified by God !

दूख रोग बिनसे भै भरम ।
साध नाम निरमल ता के करम ।।
Dukh rog binse bhai bharam.
Sadh nam nirmal ta ke karam.

सभ ते ऊच ता की सोभा बनी ।
नानक इह गुणि नामु सुखमनी ।।
Sabh te uch ta ki sobha bani.
Nanak eh gun(i) Nam(u) Sukhmani.

His sorrows, afflictions, fears
and doubts vanquished
and actions purified,
he attains sainthood !

The highest glory he acquires
(through this holy book) and
says Nanak, "This is why
it is called Sukhmani !"

BOOKS OF RELATED INTEREST

DANCING WITH THE VOID
The Innerstandings of a Rare-born Mystic
Sunyata
ISBN: 81-7822-134-9

TEN UPANISHADS OF FOUR VEDAS

Ram K. Piparaiya

ISBN: 81-7822-159-4

DIALOGUES ON REALITY
An Exploration into the Nature of Our Ultimate Identity
Robert Powell
ISBN: 81-7822-140-3

INTRODUCTION TO BUDDHISM
An Explanation of the Buddhist Way of Life
Geshe Kelsang Gyatso
ISBN: 81-7822-065-2

BHAGAVAD-GITA
Combined with his Essays on the Gita
William Quan Judge
ISBN: 81-7822-096-2

SILENCE SPEAKS

Baba Hari Dass

ISBN: 81-7822-172-1

UNCONDITIONAL BLISS
Finding Happiness in the Face of Hardship
Howard Raphael Cushnir
ISBN: 81-7822-013-x

PATH WITHOUT FORM
A Journey into the Realm Beyond Thought
Robert Powell
ISBN: 81-7822-135-7

DIVINE LIGHT
Yoga Systems with Their Secret Techniques
S.K. Das
ISBN: 81-7822-097-0

KARMA AND CHAOS
New and Collected Essays on Vipassana Meditation
Paul R. Fleischman
ISBN: 81-7822-177-2

SUPERCONSCIOUSNESS
How to Benefit from Emerging Spiritual Trends
J. Donald Walters
ISBN: 81-7822-026-1

CAN YOU LISTEN TO A WOMAN
A Man's Journey to the Heart
David Forsee
ISBN: 81-7822-112-8

THE SCIENCE OF GOD-REALIZATION
Knowing Our True Nature and Our Relationship with the Infinite
Roy Eugene Davis
ISBN: 81-7822-082-2

THE YOGI
Portraits of Swami Vishnu-devananda
Gopala Krishna
ISBN: 81-7822-038-5

BEYOND RELIGION
Meditations on Our True Nature
Robert Powell
ISBN: 81-7822-139-x

DISCOVERING THE REALM BEYOND APPEARANCE
Pointers to the Inexpressible
Robert Powell
ISBN: 81-7822-130-6

EASTERN SPIRITUALITY FOR MODERN LIFE
Exploring Buddhism, Hinduism, Taoism & Tantra
David Pond
ISBN: 81-7822-199-3

THE MATHNAWI
The Spiritual Couplets of Maulana Jalalu-'D-Dìn Muhammad I Rumi
Selected & Tr. by E.H. Whinfield
ISBN: 81-7822-168-3

THE GITA FOR THE 21ST CENTURY
Satya Prakash Agarwal
ISBN: 81-7822-153-5

UNDERSTANDING ISLAM
Frithjof Schuon
ISBN: 81-7822-151-9

THE OCEAN OF THEOSOPHY
William Q. Judge
ISBN: 81-7822-059-8

KUNDALINI YOGA
A Brief Study of Sir John Woodroffe's "The Serpent Power"
M.P. Pandit
ISBN: 81-7822-076-8

GITA FOR SUCCESS IN MODERN LIFE
From Basement to Board Room
R.S. Garg
ISBN: 81-7822-125-x

THE BODHISATTVA VOW
The Essential Practices of Mahayana Buddhism
Geshe Kelsang Gyatso
ISBN: 81-7822-067-9

35 GOLDEN KEYS TO WHO YOU ARE AND WHY YOU'RE HERE

Linda C. Anderson

ISBN: 81-7822-037-7

MYSTICAL VERSES OF A DALAI LAMA

Glenn H. Mullin

ISBN: 81-7822-117-9

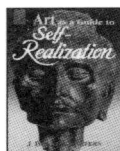
ART AS A GUIDE TO SELF-REALIZATION

J. Donald Walters

ISBN: 81-7822-028-8

MOTHER OF THE UNIVERSE
Visions of the Goddess and Tantric Hymns of Enlightenment
Lex Hixon
ISBN: 81-7822-190-x

THE SELF-REVEALED KNOWLEDGE THAT LIBERATES THE SPIRIT

Roy Eugene Davis

ISBN: 81-7822-050-4

LIVING ENLIGHTENMENT
A Call for Evolution beyond Ego

Andrew Cohen

ISBN: 81-7822-142-x

THE YOGA OF LOVE
Based on Sri Aurobindo's Synthesis of Yoga

M.P. Pandit

ISBN: 81-7822-057-1

COLLISION WITH THE INFINITE
A Life Beyond the Personal Self
Suzanne Segal **ISBN: 81-7822-113-6**

9 SECRETS OF SUCCESSFUL MEDITATION
To Trigger Spiritual Growth & Harmony in Daily Living
Samprasad Vinod
ISBN: 81-7822-137-3

SOUL POWER
The Transformation that Happens When You Know

Nikki De Carteret

ISBN: 81-7822-145-4

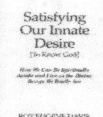
SATISFYING OUR INNATE DESIRE
How We Can be Spiritually Awake and Live as the Divine Beings We Really Are

Roy Eugene Davis

ISBN: 81-7822-198-5

THE SPIRITUAL BASIS OF REAL PROSPERITY
How to Always Be in the Flow of Resources and Supportive Events Relationships for Your Highest Good

Roy Eugene Davis

ISBN: 81-7822-053-9